VAN HUNTER VON

VOL. 1

BY
RON KAULFERSCH
AND
MIKE SCHWARK

KAPLAN

TOKYOPOP®

HAMBURG // LONDON // LOS ANGELES // TOKYO

VAN VON HUNTER

INTRODUCTION

In the dark ages long ago (or was it only three years ago?), in a war-torn land where tranquility and harmony once blossomed, tyranny ruled with a flaming fist! At last, a hero arose to defeat the evildoers and return hope to the people and peace to the countryside, albeit with mass-amnesia as an unfortunate side effect. Van Von Hunter, vanquisher of Evil Stuff, and his loyal sidekick... um... whatever-her-name-is, earned their place in the moth-eaten fabric of history, and a well-deserved break from battle.

But it appears that dark forces are back with a vengeance in the twice-peaceful land of Dikay, and in their hour of direst-est need, the commoners and a mysterious cloaked stranger once again seek a champion to right wrongs and triumph over villainy! Not even archmages and brunch buffets can long stand in the way of righteousness and the ability to point out the obvious.

Van Von Hunter Vol. 1
Created by Ron Kaulfersch and Mike Schwark

Cover Artists - Ron Kaulfersch and Mike Schwark
Kaplan Edition Writer - K. Connor Martin
Production Artists - James Dashiell, James Lee, Joe Macasocol & Mike Estacio
Additional Design - Louis Csontos
Cover Designers - Raymond Makowski and Louis Csontos
Editors - Lillian Diaz-Przybyl and Mark Paniccia

Editorial Director, Kaplan Publishing - Jennifer Farthing
Project Editor, Kaplan Publishing - Eric Titner
Production Editor, Kaplan Publishing - Fred Urfer

Digital Imaging Manager - Chris Buford
Pre-Production Supervisor - Erika Terriquez
Art Director - Anne Marie Horne
Production Manager - Elisabeth Brizzi
Managing Editor - Vy Nguyen
VP of Production - Ron Klamert
Editor-in-Chief - Rob Tokar
Publisher - Mike Kiley
President and C.O.O. - John Parker
C.E.O. and Chief Creative Officer - Stuart Levy

Published by Kaplan Publishing, a division of Kaplan, Inc.
1 Liberty Plaza, 24th Floor
New York, NY 10006

A  Manga

TOKYOPOP and 🎭 are trademarks or registered trademarks of TOKYOPOP Inc.

TOKYOPOP Inc.
5900 Wilshire Blvd. Suite 2000
Los Angeles, CA 90036

E-mail: info@TOKYOPOP.com
Come visit us online at www.TOKYOPOP.com

ISBN-13: 978-1-4277-5494-3
ISBN-10: 1-4277-5494-2
First printing: July 2007
10 9 8 7 6 5 4 3 2 1
Printed in the USA

Kaplan Publishing books are available at special quantity discounts to use for sales promotions, employee premiums, or educational purposes. Please email our Special Sales Department to order or for more information at kaplanpublishing@kaplan.com, or write to Kaplan Publishing, 1 Liberty Plaza, 24th Floor, NY, NY, 10006.

INVIOLABLE

\in VY uh lu bul\ (adj.): that
may not be broken, violated, or
assaulted

The relieved refugee, *inviolable*
under the embassy's protection,
finally settled into a deep sleep.

MANDATE

\MAN dayt\ (n.): a command or
instruction

The U.S. Marshals Service
was given a *mandate* by the
Department of Justice to pursue
and arrest federal fugitives.

LET ME TELL YOU OF THE TIME OF LEGENDS. BACK WHEN THE WORLD WAS STILL YOUNG, AND THE NEFARIOUS FORCES OF DARKNESS SOUGHT TO TAKE THE EARTH AS THEIR OWN.

NEFARIOUS

\ni FAHR ee uss\ (adj.): vicious, evil

Nefarious deeds are never far from the sinister villain's mind.

EVIL ENTERED THIS WORLD THROUGH A DEMONIC GATE ERECTED IN THE KINGDOM OF DIKAY, WHICH WAS SOON INUNDATED WITH ALL MANNER OF GHOULS, VAMPIRES AND THE UNDEAD. THE DARKNESS SUBVERTED THE LAND, AND THE KINGDOM BECAME THE CORNERSTONE OF EVIL IN THIS WORLD.

INUNDATE

\IN un dayt\ (v.): to cover with water; to overwhelm

After the press *inundated* her with requests for interviews, the author withdrew to the tranquility of her summer cottage.

SUBVERT

\sub VERT\ (v.): to undermine or corrupt

The traitor intended to *subvert* loyal citizens of the crown with the revolutionary propaganda he distributed.

ANCIENT

\AYN shent\ (adj.): very old; antiquated

The curator at the museum was almost fooled into believing that a stone sculpture made last year was actually an *ancient* Greek statue.

RESOLUTE

\REZ uh loot\ (adj.): determined; with a clear purpose

Louise was *resolute*; she would get into medical school no matter what.

IN THOSE <u>ANCIENT</u> TIMES A <u>RESOLUTE</u> CHAMPION EMERGED! HE LIVED FOR ONE PURPOSE AND ONE PURPOSE ALONE!

TO HUNT DOWN ALL THAT IS EVIL, AND <u>EXTERMINATE</u> IT!

IT WAS HE WHO <u>DEPOSED</u> THE CORRUPT PRINCE WHO HAD ENGINEERED THE ASSAULT OF THE LEGIONS OF TERROR!

EXTERMINATE

\ek STUR mu nayt\ (v.): destroy completely, annihilate

When the office manager noticed that the building was infested with vermin, he hired an expert to *exterminate* them.

DEPOSE

\dee POZ\ (v.): to remove from a high position, as from a throne

After being *deposed* from his throne, the king spent the rest of his life in exile.

IT WAS HE WHO
FOUGHT BACK THE
VILE DEMONS WHO
CLAWED THEIR WAY
HERE FROM THE
DARKEST DEPTHS OF
HELL!

AND THEN AT LAST, WHEN
THE WICKED SORCERESS
WAS ABOUT TO DESTROY
THE UNIVERSE WITH HER
ULTIMATE ATTACK, HE
OVERCAME HER AS WELL,
AND BROUGHT ABOUT
FINAL PEACE!

AND HOW
DO I KNOW OF
THESE MOMENTOUS
EVENTS, WHICH
CAME TO PASS
NEARLY 10,000
YEARS AGO, YOU
MAY ASK?

VILE

\VIYL\ (adj.):
loathsome,
disgusting,
offensive, wretched

When we worked
in the chemistry
lab we needed
to mix many of
the chemicals in
a special airshaft
that protected us
from the *vile* odors
the chemicals
produced.

OVERCOME

\oh ver KUM\ (v.): defeat, conquer

Michelle managed to *overcome* her
fears of heights to go on the tall
rollercoaster this past summer.

MOMENTOUS

\moh MEN tuss\ (adj.): very
important or significant

Choosing to quit her job to
pursue a career in acting was a
momentous decision for Louise.

I WAS THERE!

UH, GRANDPA?

THAT WAS *THREE* YEARS AGO. EVERYONE KNOWS ABOUT THAT!

YET EVEN NOW, HIS THIRST FOR VILLAINS TO DESTROY IS <u>INFINITE</u>.

EVEN NOW, HE WANDERS THE WORLD, LOOKING FOR EVIL TO SMITE!

...AND ALL THESE CENTURIES HENCE, IN THIS <u>TRANQUIL</u> WORLD, HIS LEGEND HAS <u>WANED</u>.

HEY KID!

TRANQUIL

\TRAN kwil\—
peaceful, calm,
composed

The ship's captain looked over at the *tranquil* sea, motionless in the sun's setting sky.

WANE

\WAYN\ (v.):
decline, decrease in size or intensity

The new shortstop saw his popularity begin to *wane* immediately after the serious error.

INFINITE

\IN fu nit\ (adj.): unlimited, boundless

Possessing seemingly *infinite* patience, the instructor calmly explained the relatively simple procedure for the fourth time.

ALLEVIATE

\ah LEE vee ayt\ (v.): to relieve, to improve partially

This medicine will help to *alleviate* the pain.

PERPLEX

\pir PLEKS\ (v.): to confuse

Shawna had felt sure that she would beat the crowd to the sale; the sight of so many people already in the store deeply *perplexed* her.

RAMBLE

\RAMbl\ (v.): to roam, wander; to babble, digress

Central Park was designed to allow visitors either to lounge on its lawns or to *ramble* down its various paths.

PRESERVE

\pre ZURV\ (v.): to protect, to keep unchanged

The museum keeps the ancient manuscripts locked in airtight glass containers in order to *preserve* them.

INTREPID

\in TREP id\
(adj.): fearless

The *intrepid* explorer entered the ominous-looking cave without a moment's hesitation.

BEWILDER

\be WILL der\
(v.): to confuse or puzzle

The class found themselves *bewildered* by Professor Yasmeet's lecture on advanced photonics.

CONCOCT

\kon KOKT\ (v.): to devise

When pressed for an excuse for his weeklong absence, Richard *concocted* a story so outrageous that his teacher knew he was lying.

GIBBER

\JIB ur\ (v.): to prattle unintelligibly

Cathy can't understand a word her friends say when they get excited; they start *gibbering* at incredible speeds.

YES, FOR CENTURIES YOUR FAMILY HAS ENGAGED THE FORCES OF EVIL IN AN ETERNAL <u>CONFLICT</u> OF DARK VERSES LIGHT...THE BATTLE OF GOODNESS AND EVILISHNESS!

REALLY? I HAD NO IDEA!

YES, AND NOW THE TIME HAS COME TO ACCEPT THE ROLE <u>BEQUEATHED</u> TO YOU, AND JOIN ME.

"FOR THE EVIL ONE SHALL RETURN TO <u>REVIVE</u> HIS DOMINION, AND USHER IN A NEW AGE OF DARKNESS... UNLESS THE GREAT WARRIORS OF OLD ARISE TO <u>ERADICATE</u> THIS DEMONIC PLAGUE FOR ALL ETERNITY!"

CONFLICT

\KON flikt\ (n.): a clash, a battle

The *conflict* between Debbie and Gerry heightened as the former friends began to insult each other publicly.

BEQUEATH

\bi KWEETH\ (v.): to pass on, hand down

Fred thought that his grandmother was penniless, and so was shocked when she *bequeathed* to him a beautiful gold watch.

REVIVE

\reh VIYV\ (v.): to resuscitate, bring back to life; to restore to use

The competent acting troupe *revived* interest in the theater among neighborhood residents.

ERADICATE

\ih RAD ih kayt\ (v.): to erase or wipe out

It is unlikely that poverty will ever be completely *eradicated* in this country, though the general standard of living has significantly improved in recent decades.

IS THAT WHAT THE ANCIENT PROPHECY SAYS?

NAH, JUST SOMETHING I READ ON THIS FLYER. SOMEONE SLID IT UNDER MY FRONT DOOR THIS MORNING.

IT'S ALL SO STRANGE... PLEASE EXCUSE MY SKEPTICISM, BUT--

--I DON'T THINK I CAN DO IT.

SKEPTICISM
\SKEP tih sizm\ (n.): doubt, disbelief; uncertainty

Despite their onlookers' *skepticism*, the Wright Brothers demonstrated that man was capable of flight.

I-I DON'T THINK I'D BE VERY ADEPT AT BATTLING EVIL!

SURE YOU WOULD BE! BACK BEFORE EVIL WAS BANISHED FROM DIKAY IN THE FINAL BATTLE, WE USED TO FIGHT IT ALL THE TIME.

ADEPT
\ah DEPT\ (adj.): very skilled

After fifteen years of piano practice, Lisa became *adept* at playing songs without sheet music.

BANISH
\BAN ish\ (v.): to drive away, expel

After his defeat at Waterloo, the European leaders chose to *banish* Napoleon to the remote island of Elba.

FLEE

\FLEE\ (v.): to run away from; to escape

Many of the first immigrants to North America were *fleeing* religious persecution in their home countries.

DISPEL

\dis PELL\ (v.): to drive out or scatter

Arnie's heroic rescue of the family from the flames *dispelled* any doubts that he could be a good fireman.

OUTCAST

\OWT kast\ (n.): someone rejected from a society

The *outcast* decided that the only way to rejoin the group was to give in to their demands.

RELY

\re LIY\ (v.): to be
dependant on; to
have confidence in

The Delta Force
relied on the
intelligence
supplied to them by
satellite, and were
forced to pull back
when they lost their
connection.

SQUANDER

\SKWAN der\ (v.): to waste

While I've been saving for a
piano, my friend Sean has been
squandering all his earnings on
lottery tickets.

VILLAINOUS

\VIL uh nus\ (adj.): offensive,
obnoxious, wicked

When the public learned of the duke's
villainous plot to overthrow the king,
they stormed his home and dragged
him straight to the royal palace.

CHAPTER 2!

(YES, WE KNOW WE'RE YELLING!)

PUNCTUAL

\PUNK shoo ull\
(adj.): on time

Barbara was surprised that the train came late today because it was usually so *punctual*.

> I TOLD YOU TO BE PUNCTUAL-- YOU'VE GOT TO BE HERE FIRST THING IN THE MORNING! IT'S ALREADY 6:15. SINCE YOU WERE NEGLIGENT, I HAD TO HIRE YOUR REPLACE-MENT.

> WH--WHO'S THIS?

NEGLIGENT

\NEG lih jent\
(adj.): careless, inattentive

The court determined that Mr. Glass had been *negligent* in failing to keep his vicious dog chained up.

> WHAT DO YOU MEAN?! I WAS ONLY FIFTEEN...

THRONG

\THRONG\ (n.): a large group of people, crowd

Glenda squeezed through the *throngs* of people trying to reach the box office before it closed.

> WAIT--ARE YOU SAYING THERE ARE THRONGS OF CUSTOMERS AT 6 AM?!?

> SOME CLIENTELE! WHAT KIND OF PATHETIC, LOWLIFE DRUNKARD WOULD BE HERE THIS EARLY IN THE...

> SO WHAT CAN I GET YOU?

> SCOTCH. NEAT.

CLIENTELE

\kly en TELL\ (n.): a body of customers or patrons

Le Caravelle, one of the most expensive restaurants in the city, caters to a wealthy *clientele*.

PATHETIC

\puh THET ik\ (adj.): arousing scornful pity

The judges could not believe that anyone would submit such a *pathetic* exhibit and were forced to reject the artist from the competition.

24

AH, A PAYING CUSTOMER. SO HAVE A SEAT, AND TELL ME YOUR PROBLEMS.

SIGH

HAVE YOU EVER HAD ONE OF THOSE DAYS WHERE IT'S <u>DISCLOSED</u> TO YOU THAT PERHAPS THE *ONLY* WAY TO CURE YOURSELF OF THE AMNESIA THAT'S PLAGUED YOU FOR *THREE YEARS* IS TO JOIN UP WITH SOMEONE WHO CLAIMS HE KNEW YOU FROM YOUR PAST, AND WANTS TO TAKE YOU STRAIGHT INTO THE PATH OF *DANGER* IN ORDER TO STOP AN <u>APPALLING</u> EVIL FROM BEING REBORN?

DISCLOSE

\dis CLOZ\ (v.):
to make known,
expose to view

The reporter refused to *disclose* the sources mentioned in his article, bound as he was to preserve their anonymity.

APPALLING

uh PAW ling\ (adj.): causing
dismay, frightful

The amount of cheating that goes on in today's high schools is absolutely *appalling*.

CONTAGIOUS

\kon TAY jus\
(adj.): spreading
from one to
another

Lucy was ordered
by the doctor
to stay home
until her disease
was no longer
contagious.

FORLORN

\for LORN\ (adj.):
dreary, deserted,
unhappy, hopeless

Ying felt *forlorn*
at the prospect of
moving out of the
house in which she
had been born.

EONS AGO, I WAS A POWERFUL *GOD* OF THE UNDERWORLD...

BUT I WAS BOUND INTO HUMAN FORM AND MADE TO FORGET WHO I *TRULY* WAS!

BUT YES! AS MY MEMORY RETURNS, MY POWERS ARE *UNFETTERED!*

HA! NOW I SHALL RULE YOU PITIFUL MORTALS WITH SUCH *BRUTALITY* THAT...

UNFETTER

\un FET er\ (v.): to free from restrictions

The dog owners fighting the ordinance believe they should have the right to *unfetter* their dogs occasionally, rather than keep them on leashes at all times.

BRUTALITY

\broo TAL ih tee\ (n.): ruthless, cruel, and unrelenting acts

The *brutality* of the locust plague overwhelmed the farmers as it destroyed a whole year's crop.

COHERENT

\ko HEE rent\ (adj.): intelligible, lucid, understandable

Cathy was so tired that her speech was barely *coherent*.

ELIMINATE

\ee LIM uh nayt\ (v.): to get rid of, remove

One of television's first reality shows placed a group of strangers on an island and forced them to *eliminate* a contestant each week until there was only one person left.

DEMOLISH

\de MOL ish\ (v.): to destroy; to damage severely

Before starting construction on the new skyscraper, workers will have to *demolish* the old buildings that still sit on the site.

FATHOM

\FAH thom\ (v.): to comprehend, penetrate the meaning of

Andrea couldn't *fathom* how a person could cheat on a test; every instinct told her it was wrong.

UM... MASTER?

I'M RELUCTANT TO QUESTION YOU BUT...

WE'VE JUST BEEN STANDING HERE FOR THE PAST TWO HOURS.

YES, WELL...

I JUST REALIZED...

I HAVE ABSOLUTELY *NO* IDEA WHERE WE'RE GOING.

RELUCTANT

\re LUK tant\ (adj.): unwilling, opposing; hesitant

Florence was *reluctant* to believe the weather report that called for snow; the news had been wrong too often in the past.

PROCURE

\pro KYOOR\ (v.): to acquire, obtain; to get

The evidence was inadmissible in court because the police officer did not *procure* it legally.

HEHEHEHEHE HEHEHEHE

YOU HEAR THAT?

IT'S JUST THE WIND, MOCKING AND TAUNTING US.

THE DARK ONE DEPOSED, BUT NOT YET GONE, POWER HE SEEKS, SO HIS REIGN MAY GO ON!

IN THE DARKEST DEPTHS THE BLACK EYE LIES, IN A CLANDESTINE SPOT KNOWN ONLY TO I!

A FORMER-PRINCE, WHOSE FAVORITE COLOR IS ORANGE, UNPARALLELED EVIL SHALL BRING, WHEN HE...

MOCK

\MOK\ (v.): to deride, ridicule

Charles suspected that Toni was *mocking* him behind his back, but in fact, she respected him greatly.

TAUNT

\TAWNT\ (v.): to ridicule; to mock, insult

Gary sat crying in a corner of the playground because the other children had *taunted* him for wearing pink polka dot suspenders.

UNPARALLELED

\un PAR uh leld\ (adj.): unequaled; without match

To many, Michael Jordan was an *unparalleled* athlete who redefined basketball stardom.

CLANDESTINE

\klan DES tin\ (adj.): secretive, concealed for a darker purpose

The double agent paid many *clandestine* visits to the president's office in the dead of the night.

ATTAIN

\uh TAYN\ (v.): to accomplish, gain

It is clear that Clem's hard work will help him *attain* that raise he's been hoping for.

BLAZE

\BLAYZ\ (v.): to shine brightly; to flare up suddenly

The fire *blazed* through the night, providing heat and light to the campers as they slept.

I CAN SHOW YOU THE WAY TO THE ITEM WHICH SHALL UNLEASH ULTIMATE DARKNESS UPON THE WORLD.

AH, EXCELLENT. LEAD ON...

DOESN'T HE SEEM A LITTLE...*DEVIOUS*, MY MASTER?

NOT AT ALL!

HE'S A CUTE LITTLE HALF-DECAYED JESTER, WAITING FOR US ON THE OUTSKIRTS OF THE DARK FOREST. THAT'S NOTHING TO BE *WARY* OF.

ACTUALLY, I'D SAY IT'S *SERENDIPITY*!

THIS WAY! THIS WAY!

DEVIOUS

\DEE vee us\ (adj.): shifty, not straightforward

No one would realize how *devious* Sue Ann had been until the damage from her secret plotting was revealed.

WARY

\WAYR ee\ (adj.): careful, cautious

The dog was *wary* of Barney at first, only gradually letting its guard down and wagging its tail.

SERENDIPITY

\se ren DIP ih tee\ (n.): the tendency to make fortunate discoveries by chance

Rosemary's *serendipity* revealed itself in many ways, such as her habit of finding money on the street.

WHO *IS* THAT?!?

HAVEN'T A <u>NOTION</u>.

NOTION

\NO shin\ (n.):
idea or conception

Mandatory school uniforms is a *notion* that has been tossed back and forth in governments, but has never been implemented on a national scale in the United States.

BUT WHEN SOMEONE SHOWS UP <u>SHROUDED</u> IN A HUGE, <u>AMORPHOUS</u> CLOAK, YOU KNOW SOME SERIOUS STUFF IS ABOUT TO GO DOWN.

AMORPHOUS

\ah MOR fus\ (adj.): having no definite form

The movie The Blob featured an *amorphous* creature that was constantly changing shape.

SHROUD

\SHROWD\ (v.): to shut off from sight

The wizard used his powers to bring down a dense cloud which *shrouded* the village in mist.

35

CAJOLE

ka JOL\ (v.): to flatter, coax, or persuade

The spoiled girl could *cajole* her father into buying her anything.

ENORMOUS

\ee NOR muss\ (adj.): very great in size or degree

The *enormous* sculpture of the elephant dwarfed the delighted children.

ECCENTRIC

\ek SEN trik\ (adj.): abnormal, unconventional

Many people like to joke that poor people are called crazy while rich people are only referred to as *eccentric*.

OH, HIM! YEAH, RUMOR HAS IT THAT HE MAY BE THAT CELEBRATED HERO OF LEGEND, THE BANE OF EVILDOERS, WHO DEFEATED THE FORCES OF DARKNESS NEARLY TEN THOUSAND YEARS AGO!

NO ONE'S SEEN THE MAN SINCE ANCIENT TIMES. HELL, WE DON'T EVEN KNOW WHAT HE LOOKS LIKE!

OH, HE'S RIGHT AT THE END OF THE BAR, EAVESDROPPING ON US.

I'M FAIRLY CONFIDENT THAT IT WAS THREE YEARS AGO.

CELEBRATED

\SELL uh bray ted\ (adj.): known and praised widely

The class quivered with excitement in anticipation of the *celebrated* author's upcoming speech.

BANE

\BAYN\ (n.): a cause of harm or ruin; a source of annoyance

Speeches were the *bane* of Jenny's existence; she hated having to stand up in front of a crowd.

CONFIDENT

\KON fi dent\ (adj.): certain, self-assured

Confident that she was going to ace the exam, Cynthia strode into class with a broad smile across her face.

REHASH

\re HASH\ (v.): to bring forth again with no real change

Timmy didn't want to do any new work, so he decided to *rehash* the paper he had written for last year's course, hoping his teacher wouldn't notice.

DISHEVELED

\di SHEV uld\ (adj.): marked by disorder, untidy, messy

The teacher noted the student's *disheveled* appearance and sent him into the hall to neaten up.

PROHIBIT

\pro HIB it\ (v.): to forbid, prevent

Marge's parents *prohibited* her from attending her senior prom because they thought dancing was immoral.

HERE WE ARE!

WOW. IT'S VAST.

CHAPTER 3
(WOW. THIS IS A REALLY SMALL SUBTITLE.)

THE VON HUNTER FAMILY FIRST ACQUIRED THIS ESTATE GENERATIONS AGO...

UM...

Von Hunter
VAUGHN ESTATE

YEAH, WELL...UH... WHO SAYS NAMES HAVE TO BE INVARIABLE? WE'RE THE VON HUNTERS NOW.

YOU DO REALIZE THE PLAQUE SAYS "VAUGHN ESTATE," RIGHT?

HEH...

VAST

\VAST\ (adj.): immense, enormous, great in size or intensity

Because of her *vast* knowledge of random trivia, Margaret was an expert game show contestant.

ACQUIRE

\ah KWIYR\ (v.): to gain possession of

After this weekend's movie marathon, Lenora *acquired* a taste for Italian movies.

INVARIABLE

\in VAR ee uh bul\ (adj.): constant, unchanging

To protect the integrity of the chemical, we must keep it in a sealed room with *invariable* temperature.

DON'T SEEM TO...UH... HAVE THE KEYS.

?

THIS WHOLE STORY WOULDN'T HAPPEN TO BE **FABRICATED**, WOULD IT?

OH, C'MON ALREADY! OPEN UP!

LIKE ABOUT THAT BIRTHRIGHT THING, AND ACTUALLY KNOWING WHO I AM?

THEY CAN JUST UNLOCK IT FROM THE INSIDE! GIVE ME A BREAK!

...

OKAY, SO THE DETAILS, MAY BE A LITTLE **INDISTINCT** TO ME, BUT WE REALLY DID FIGHT EVIL TOGETHER.

FABRICATED

\fab rih KAY tid\ (adj.): constructed, invented; faked, falsified

The reporter was disgraced when it was uncovered that the stories he'd published were largely *fabricated*.

INDISTINCT

\in dis TINKT\ (adj.): vague, unclear

After years of living in Europe, Athena's memories of home grew more and more *indistinct*.

PERTINENT

\PIR tih nent\ (adj.): applicable, appropriate

The supervisor felt that his employee's complaints were *pertinent* and mentioned them in the meeting.

ABSORB

\ab ZORB\ (v.): to soak up, consume; to occupy completely

Jason completely forgot to watch the baseball game, as he was too *absorbed* in his studies.

CLARITY

\KLAR it ee\ (n.): clearness; clear understanding

Henrietta explained the plan to Greg with the utmost *clarity*, but he still failed to understand.

43

PRETTY BELATED RESPONSE THERE, WALTER.

SORRY SIR, WE DIDN'T THINK YOU'D RETURN SO ABRUPTLY.

AH. SO GOOD TO SEE YOU AGAIN, MADAM.

BELATED

\bee LAY tid\ (adj.): delayed, done too late

Although Sara initially forgot her brother's birthday, she sent a *belated* card to him the following week.

ABRUPT

\ab RUPT\ (adj.): sudden; curt

The lion was thrown off guard by the *abrupt* change in direction of the elk herd.

ASSIDUOUS

\uh SI joo iss\ (adj.): diligent, persistent, hardworking

The chauffer scrubbed the limousine *assiduously*, hoping to make a good impression on his employer.

PREDICTABLE

\pre DIKT uh bul\ (adj.): expected beforehand; unsurprising

Tired of silly, *predictable* movies, the studio decided to hire a screenwriter to devise an original story that defied all expectations.

METICULOUS

\meh TIK yoo luss\ (adj.): extremely careful, fastidious, painstaking

To find all the clues at the crime scene, the investigators *meticulously* examined every inch of the area.

45

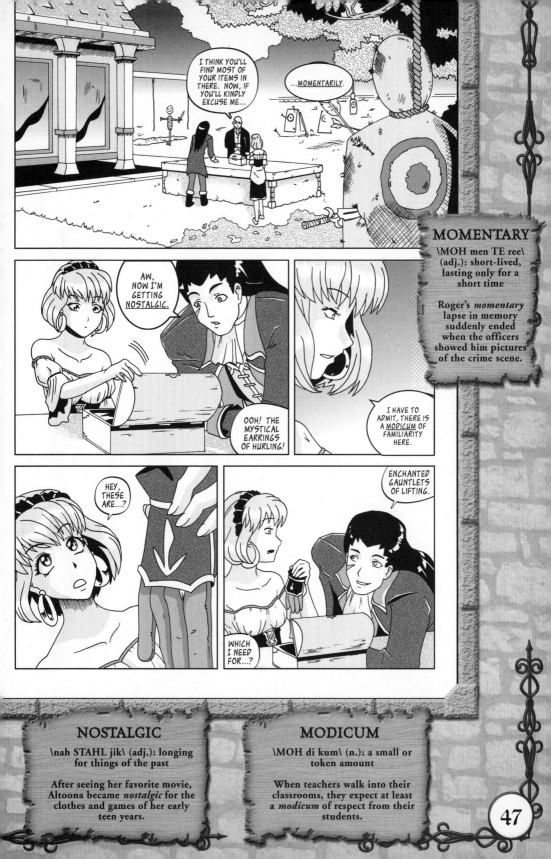

MOMENTARY
\MOH men TE ree\ (adj.): short-lived, lasting only for a short time

Roger's *momentary* lapse in memory suddenly ended when the officers showed him pictures of the crime scene.

NOSTALGIC
\nah STAHL jik\ (adj.): longing for things of the past

After seeing her favorite movie, Altoona became *nostalgic* for the clothes and games of her early teen years.

MODICUM
\MOH di kum\ (n.): a small or token amount

When teachers walk into their classrooms, they expect at least a *modicum* of respect from their students.

47

I BELIEVE YOU'LL BE NEEDING THEM TO HOIST THIS.

HOIST

\HOYST\ (v.): to lift, raise

Sam backed the pickup truck to the shed and *hoisted* the wooden crate into the back.

THE REDEATHILIZER-19, SUPER ANTI-MIDIAN CROSSBOW.

IT PROPELS SILVER-TIPPED BOLTS OVER THREE FEET IN LENGTH.

I DARE SAY IF THIS WEAPON IS HANDLED PROPERLY, EVEN THE MOST POWERFUL OPPONENT WILL SUCCUMB.

PROPEL

\pro PEL\ (v.): to cause to move forward

"Our new ideas will *propel* this company into the next century," the executive promised.

OPPONENT

\uh POH nent\ (n.): an enemy

Although the last person she debated against was a novice, Shelley knew that her next *opponent* had won the competition three years in a row.

SUCCUMB

su KUM\ (v.): to give in to stronger power; to yield

Although the small band of warriors was clearly outnumbered, they refused to *succumb* to their enemies.

INORDINATE

\in OR di net\
(adj.): excessive, immoderate

The group was deluged by an *inordinate* number of emails complaining about their newest products.

HINDRANCE

\HIN drens\ (n.): an impediment; a stumbling block

Not wishing to be a *hindrance* while their mother was preparing for the party, the children packed a picnic lunch and went to the park.

DRAWBACK

\DRAW back\ (n.): a disadvantage, an inconvenience

The *drawback* to being famous is not having any privacy when you go out in public.

GARGANTUAN

\gar GAN shoo in\ (adj.): giant, tremendous

Cleaning a teenager's room can often be a *gargantuan* task.

FRIVOLOUS

\FRIV uh luss\
(adj.): silly,
flippant, petty,
trivial

The biggest
problem in the
world for the
frivolous debutante
was that her ribbon
was the wrong
color.

VULGAR

\VUL ger\
(adj.): crudely
indecent, boorish,
ostentatious

Samantha refused
to eat a meal with
Howard again;
she found his
vulgar jokes to be
offensive.

FELICITOUS

\feh LIH sih tus\ (adj.): suitable,
appropriate; well-chosen

The father of the bride made a
felicitous speech at the wedding,
contributing to the success of the
evening.

ADVANTAGEOUS

\ADD van TAY jus\ (adj.):
favorable, useful

Derek found his Spanish-speaking
skills to be *advantageous* in his
travels to Mexico.

51

DISCOMFIT

\dis KUM fit\ (v.): to make uneasy,
embarrass

The principal was afraid the
fire drill would *discomfit* some
students, so he let the younger
classes leave the assembly early.

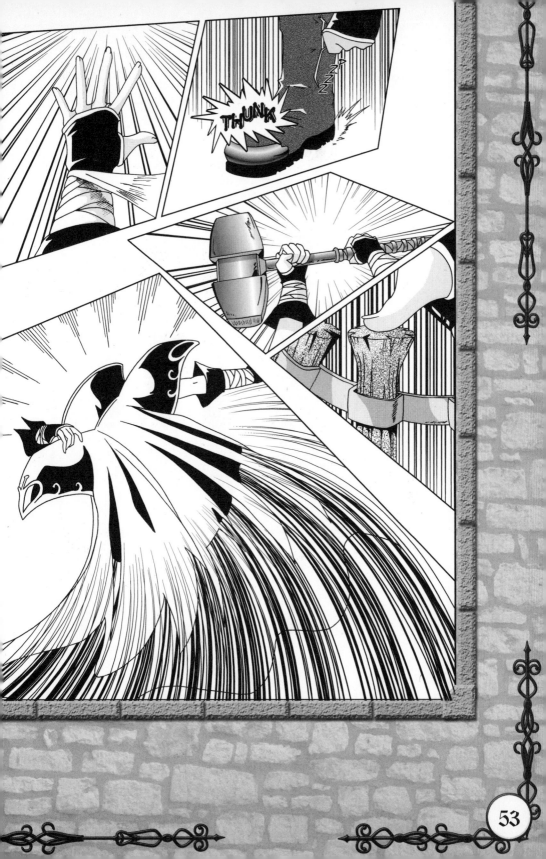

NOW THEN! I'M OFF TER SCRUB *THE TOILETS!*

UH, YEAH... I'M GOING TO HAVE TO <u>REQUISITION</u> ALL THAT STUFF.

SORRY!

REQUISITION

\re kwi ZIH shun\ (v.): to demand the use of

General Montgomery *requisitioned* a new jeep to drive from his barracks to his office.

SCOUR

\SKOWER\ (v.): to scrub clean

When Kelly discovered that her in-laws were coming to visit, she *scoured* the house in an attempt to impress them.

NITPICK

\NIT pik\ (v.): to criticize minor details

Unable to find fault with the general behavior of the company, the difficult stockholder decided instead to *nitpick* and pointed out misspellings in its correspondence.

MISCONCEPTION

\mis kon SEP shun\ (n.): an error in understanding

It is a common *misconception* that antiques are only valuable because they are old; in reality, valuable antiques are usually examples of excellent craftsmanship from their respective eras.

ASYLUM

\uh SY lum\ (n.): a place offering protection and safety; (also) an institution for the mentally ill

Many of the immigrants to the United States in the early part of the twentieth century sought *asylum* from government persecution.

PREVENT

\pre VENT\ (v.): to stop; to keep from happening

The Panthers tried their best, but they could not *prevent* the Patriots from winning the Super Bowl again.

MISSIVE

\MIS iv\ (n.): a note or letter

Lydia spent hours composing a romantic *missive* for Leo, which she sent off in the evening mail.

VACANT

\VAY kent\ (adj.): empty, unoccupied

Although several rooms at the motel were *vacant*, the owner refused to allow the suspicious couple to rent a room for the night.

SUFFICE

\suh FIYS\ (v.): to meet requirements, to be sufficient

Although I would have liked to meet with the vice president of production, the vice president of marketing will *suffice*.

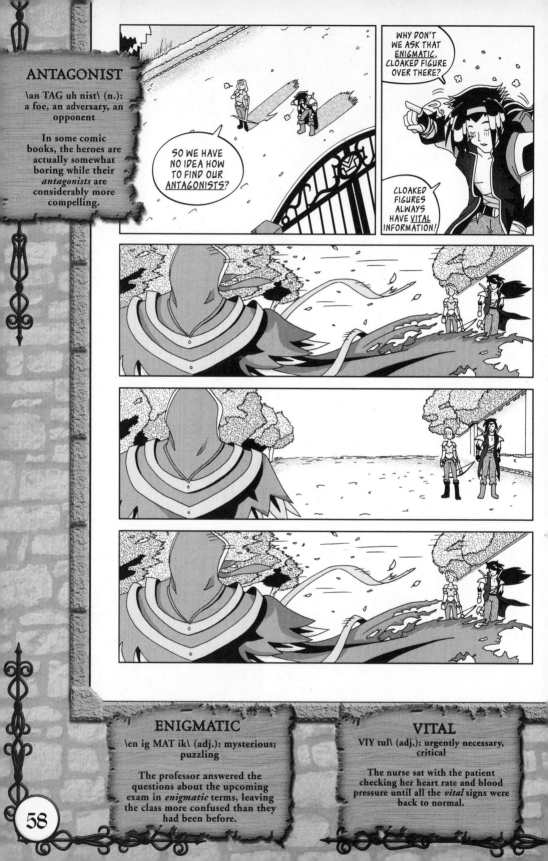

ANTAGONIST

\an TAG uh nist\ (n.):
a foe, an adversary, an
opponent

In some comic
books, the heroes are
actually somewhat
boring while their
antagonists are
considerably more
compelling.

ENIGMATIC

\en ig MAT ik\ (adj.): mysterious;
puzzling

The professor answered the
questions about the upcoming
exam in *enigmatic* terms, leaving
the class more confused than they
had been before.

VITAL

VIY tul\ (adj.): urgently necessary,
critical

The nurse sat with the patient
checking her heart rate and blood
pressure until all the *vital* signs were
back to normal.

WOOOOSH

OH NO, MY EXTRAVAGANT CLOAK!

EH, WE'RE NEVER GOING TO SEE *THAT* THING AGAIN.

LET'S PLAY HIDE AND SEEK. JULIE *SUCKS* AT THAT GAME.

EXTRAVAGANT
\ek STRAV uh gent\ (adj.): lavish

Among other *extravagant* demands, the hotel guest insisted on bathing in mineral spring water.

CHAPTER 4

(I'M REALLY RUNNING LOW ON SUBTITLE IDEAS NOW.)

INACCURATE

\in AK yur it\ (adj.): mistaken, incorrect

Jean's guesses at Lois's age were completely *inaccurate*, so Lois finally told her the truth.

ABBREVIATE

\uh BREE vee ayt\ (v.): to make shorter

When the speaker saw that her time was running short, she decided to *abbreviate* her remarks.

URGE

\URJ\ (v.): to impel, to exhort, spur to action

Principal Slater gave a passionate speech *urging* all students to take their schoolwork seriously.

RENEW

\re NOO\ (v.): resume, reaffirm, replenish

After a tense month of arguing, the two best friends *renewed* their pact to equally share the cost of maintaining the apartment.

RUTHLESS

\ROOTH less\ (adj.): merciless, compassionless

The Terminator was a perfectly *ruthless* killer, not possessing any emotions or compassion for its victims.

EBB

\EBB\ (v.): to fade away, recede

Melissa realized that she had been studying too long, because her ability to concentrate had begun to *ebb*.

CALAMITY

\ka LAM uh tee\ (n.): disaster, catastrophe

Last year's formal dance was a *calamity*; the band was an hour late and the food was spoiled.

IMPLAUSIBLE

\im PLAWS uh bul\ (adj.): improbable, inconceivable

A skeptical man by nature, Max found his neighbor's claim that he'd seen a UFO highly *implausible*.

AWE

\AW\ (n.): reverence, respect, wonder

Glenn watched in *awe* as Michael slam-dunked the basketball over Scottie's head.

AUGMENT

\awg MENT\ (v.): to expand, extend

Ben looked to *augment* his salary by applying for extra overtime hours.

FACTUAL

\FAK choo ul\ (adj.): real, true

"I have *factual* evidence that this man committed the crime!" declared the prosecuting attorney.

CONVENIENT

\kon VEEN yent\ (adj.): favorable to one's comfort or needs

The hardest part about working with a big group is finding a time that is *convenient* for everyone.

EVADE

\ee VAYD\ (v.): to avoid, dodge

He *evaded* my question by pretending not to hear me and changing the subject.

CONVEY

\kon VAY\ (v.): to transport; to make known

The goal of the game is to *convey* a phrase to your teammates without using words.

IRIDESCENT

\ih ri DES ent\ (adj.): showing
many lustrous colors

The tourists, used to the dull
colors of home, marveled at the
iridescent tropical butterfly.

ENCHANT

\en CHANT\ (v.): to attract and
delight

Lorna was dazzled by her first visit
to the Museum of Modern Art; the
brilliant colors and bold paintings
enchanted her.

SCURRY

\SKUR ree\ (v.): to scamper, to run lightly

Robin had trouble sleeping through the noise of squirrels *scurrying* across the roof.

SCOUNDREL

\SKOWN drul\ (n.): a villain, a rogue

George the Pirate was the meanest *scoundrel* ever to roam the seas.

MANIFEST

\MAN ih fest\ (adj.): perceptible, evident, obvious

The fact that she had plastic surgery done was *manifest*, since she looked 20 years younger than she had looked the week before.

AAH! SHE WORMS HER WAY INTO MY VERY SOUL WITH HER *INSIDIOUS* TELEPATHY, AND KNOWS MY MOST *PROFOUND* DESIRES!

UM... NO, ACTUALLY, THAT LITTLE FELLOW OVER THERE TOLD ME.

OH. *DISREGARD* WHAT I JUST SAID, THEN.

RIIIIGHT. COME INSIDE THEN.

INSIDIOU

\in SID ee us\ (adj.) subtly spreading harm; underhanded, cunning

Coleman's career was eventually destroyed by the *insidious* rumors that he had falsified data in his groundbreaking experiments.

PROFOUND

\pro FOWND\ (adj.): deep, meaningful; far-reaching

The audience sat silently listening to the *profound* ideas of the brilliant philosopher.

DISREGARD

\dis rih GARD\ (v.): to ignore

The building manager knew that people were going to *disregard* the "Do Not Enter" sign, so he put a security guard in front of the broken elevator.

DELINEATE

\de LIN ee ayt\ (v.): to portray, depict, describe

The coach had *delineated* the team strategy to reporters before the game.

RELEVANCE

\REL uh vens\ (n.): pertinence to the matter at hand, applicability

Because the witness's testimony bore no *relevance* to the trial, the jury was instructed to disregard it.

VIGILANT

\VIJ uh lent\ (adj.): attentive, watchful

Our community members must remain *vigilant* if we are to discover the identities of the vandals.

COLLUSION

\ku LOO zhen\ (n.): collaboration, complicity, conspiracy

It came to light that the police chief and the mafia were in *collusion* in running the numbers racket.

EXPLANATORY

\ek SPLAN uh tor ee\ (adj.): serving to make clear

Before going into detail about her project, Leeann wrote an *explanatory* section to outline her ideas.

EXPERTISE

\ek spur TEEZ\ (adj.): skill or knowledge in a particular area

In questions about grammar, I usually defer to Eileen; her *expertise* in the area outweighs my own.

MANUAL

\MAN yoo ul\ (n.): a small
instruction book

Before operating heavy machinery,
it's important to carefully read the
manual to ensure that all safety
precautions have been taken.

THWART

\THWART\ (v.): to block or prevent
from happening; to frustrate

After the tricky winds *thwarted* his
attempts to throw the bag into the
box, the chimp retired to the back of
his cage in frustration.

PREAMBLE

\PRE am bul\
(n.): introductory
passage

The *preamble* to
the Constitution
begins with the
famous phrase,
"We the People
of the United
States..."

VENERABLE

\VEN er a bul\
(adj.): respected
because of age

All the villagers
sought the
venerable old
woman's advice
whenever they
had a problem.

FORTITUDE

\FOR ti tood\ (n.):
strength of mind

Although Michelle
had the *fortitude*
to endure a six-
hour meeting, she
nonetheless agreed
to break it into
two three-hour
sessions.

ENDURE

\en DYOOR\ (v.): to carry on
despite hardships

Skiing is an exciting and
invigorating sport for those who
can *endure* being out in the cold
all day.

DIVULGE

\di VULJ\ (v.): to make known

Pat was fired for *divulging*
company secrets to its
competitors.

CATASTROPHIC

\kat uh STROF ik\ (adj.): of, or relating to, a terrible event or complete failure

If the train conductor can't stop the out-of-control train before it reaches the broken bridge, the results will be *catastrophic*.

EVALUATE

\ee VAL yoo ayt\ (v.): to examine or judge carefully

The judge instructed the jury to carefully *evaluate* all the evidence before coming to a conclusion.

AUDACIOUS

\aw DAY shus\
(adj.): bold, daring,
fearless

The protestors'
audacious slogans
angered the large
corporation, but
also won them
considerable
attention and
support from
onlookers.

DAUNTING

\DAWN ting\ (adj.): intimidating

While running the New York
Marathon may be a *daunting* task
to some, the event consistently
draws thousands of participants.

ANALYZE

\AN ah liyz\ (v.): to examine
methodically

The forensics experts brought the
blood back from the crime scene
in order to *analyze* it.

IT'S OUR **HYPOTHESIS** THAT THIS IS THE SANDWICH SPOKEN OF IN THE **PROPHETIC** LEGENDS. WE BELIEVE IT WAS FORGED ALMOST A THOUSAND YEARS AGO, BY THE DARK MASTER HIMSELF!

AND...WHICH DARK MASTER WAS THAT?

FRANKLY, WE'RE **STUMPED.**

IT'S A MOOT POINT.

HYPOTHESIS

\hi POTH a siss\ (n.): an assumption, a theory requiring proof

While the board found the researcher's *hypothesis* compelling, they simply couldn't adequately fund the experiment.

PROPHETIC

\pro FET ik\ (adj.): foretelling events by divine means

The financial officer's warnings to the board of trustees proved *prophetic* as the company sank into bankruptcy.

STUMP

\STUMP\ (v.): to baffle; to challenge

We tried hard, but we were unable to *stump* Nate with sports trivia.

CLAIRVOYANCE

\klayr VOY ens\ (adj.): exceptionally insightful, able to foresee the future

His *clairvoyance* allowed him a clear vision of the company's imminent success.

INDISCRIMINATE

\in dis KRIM uh nit\ (adj.): not based on careful distinctions, chaotic

The director chose his cast *indiscriminately*, utilizing the first twenty people to answer his audition call, regardless of their abilities or experience.

YES, THE EBON EYE IS IN MY POSSESSION. BUT YOU ARE NOT THE ONLY ONE WHO SEEKS IT. MY POWERS OF CLAIRVOYANCE REVEAL ANOTHER... A MAN KNOWN AS VON, THE VAN HUNTER.

VAN VON HUNTER?!

CLOSE ENOUGH.

OH NO, NOT HIM! THAT MAN KILLS EVIL INDISCRIMINATELY. THIS COULD BE A PROBLEM.

AH, BUT YOU ARE THE FIRST TO COME TO ME... AS THE MYSTIC SANDS IN THIS HOURGLASS HAVE FALLEN FOR A THOUSAND YEARS, SO HAVE I LIVED ON TO ADMINISTER DEMANDING TESTS TO ALL WHO WOULD DARE TO EXPLOIT THE DARK POWERS OF THE EBON EYE.

DEMANDING

\de MAN ding\ (adj.): requiring much effort and attention

Joe had to quit his part-time job in order to keep up with his *demanding* schedule at school.

EXPLOIT

\ek SPLOYT\ (v.): to take advantage of

The brilliant tactician studied his enemy's methods to discover a weakness that he could easily *exploit* in battle.

IF YOU CAN COMPLETE THESE TASKS-- WITH ALACRITY-- IT SHALL BE YOURS! FIRST, I TASK THEE WITH...

CRUNCH SNAP MUNCH MUNCH MUNCH!

?

DID...YOU JUST EAT MY ARM?

MRUHMNH... HUNGRY.

YAAAAAAAAAH! MUNCHMUNCHMUNCH

ALACRITY

\ah LACK ri tee\ (n.): cheerful
willingness, eagerness; speed

The eager dog obeyed with great
alacrity, fetching the stick that
had been tossed for him.

EXEMPLARY

\egg ZEM pluh ree\ (adj.): outstanding, an example to others

His *exemplary* behavior was a model for the rest of the class.

ENCROACH

\en KROHCH\ (v.): to impinge, infringe, intrude upon

Some environmentalists are concerned that as the human population expands, we continually *encroach* on natural habitats like the rainforests.

SQUELCH

\SKWELCH\ (v.): to suppress, to put down with force

Despite the reformer's best efforts, the company board of directors *squelched* all attempts to change office policy.

GLUTTON

\GLUT in\ (n.):
a person who
eats and drinks
excessively

Only a *glutton*
could order
dessert after such
a rich meal.

DEVOUR

\di VOWR\ (v.): to eat greedily,
consume

Robert was so hungry after his bike
race that he *devoured* an entire
pizza.

CARNIVOROUS

\kar NIV uh riss\ (adj.): meat-
eating

Dogs, since they are *carnivorous*
animals, generally do not do well
on purely vegetarian diets.

79

CHAPTER 5

(WE'RE STILL PUTTING IN SUBTITLES? OH, SON OF A...)

THIS WAIT IS INTERMINABLE.

HEY, IF HE IS DEAD, DO I REALLY HAVE TO KEEP SITTING HERE?

THE TRIAL WOULD EXCEED THE ENDURANCE OF MERE MORTALS, BUT IT IS MY CONVICTION THAT VAN IS THE HERO OF LEGEND. SURELY HE CAN PASS THE TEST.

GREAT. SO WE PERSEVERE WITH THE WAITING, THEN.

INTERMINABLE

\in TER mi nu bul\ (adj.): endless

By the time the *interminable* play ended, the last train home had already left.

ENDURANCE

\en DOOR uns\ (n.): ability to withstand hardships

To prepare for the marathon, Bekki built up her *endurance* by running ten miles every day.

CONVICTION

\kon VIC shun\ (n.): a fixed or strong belief

Sally would not be swayed from her *conviction* that the best color for a sports car is red.

PERSEVERE

\pir suh VEER\ (v.): to refuse to stop, regardless of difficulty

Gail *persevered* and trekked through three feet of snow to visit her sick uncle.

PREDOMINANT

\pre DOM ih nunt\ (adj.): most important or conspicuous

While many creatures inhabit J.R.R. Tolkien's Middle Earth, elves are the most *predominant* figures in the early history of the world.

VICARIOUS

\viy KAYR ee us\ (adj.): experienced secondhand

Although Yuri had never traveled outside his hometown, he felt *vicarious* thrills of adventure through the many novels he read.

LOOKS LIKE MY "LIFE OF ADVENTURE" IS GOING TO HAVE TO BE <u>PREDOMINANTLY VICARIOUS</u>.

OH, SO THE KIZIK GIRL HAS ALREADY <u>PRODDED</u> THE HEROES TO COME THIS FAR, HMM? EXCELLENT!

MY <u>CUNNING</u> PLAN IS FALLING INTO PLACE. I AM THE PUPPET MASTER!

PROD

\PROD\ (v.): to poke or nudge; to persuade

When the dog fell asleep in the doorway, the child kept *prodding* it to wake up and move.

CUNNING

\KUN ing\ (adj.): characterized by artful deception; clever

The *cunning* general devised a way to outsmart both his opponents and force them to fight each other.

BOAST

\BOHST\ (v.): to speak with
excessive pride

"I can beat all of you at that
video game any day of the week,"
boasted Derrick.

83

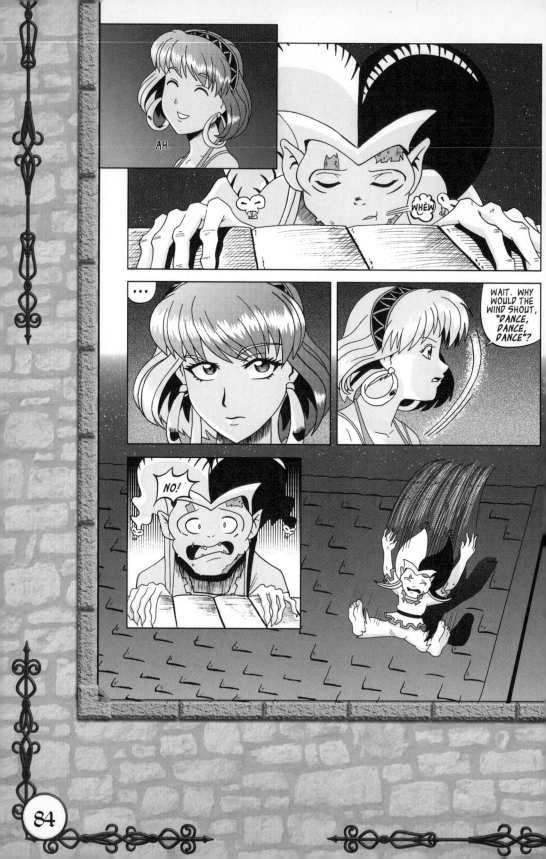

INVESTIGATE

\in VEST ih gayt\ (v.): to examine,
to look into

Insurance companies hire agents
to check claims and *investigate*
their validity.

PROCRASTINATE

\pro KRAS tih nayt\ (v.): to put off doing work

Zack tried to *procrastinate* as long as possible, but knew that he would have to hand in his assignment eventually.

NAÏVE

\nye EEV\ (adj.): lacking experience and understanding

Although the newly elected politician was very *naïve* about political maneuvering in Washington, it only took her a few weeks to learn the tricks of Congress.

FLAGRANT

\FLAY grent\ (adj.): outrageous, shameless

His *flagrant* disregard for company policy resulted in his dismissal from the job.

PLOY

\PLOY\ (n.): maneuver, plan

To catch the con artist, the detective developed a *ploy* whereby the criminal himself would admit his guilt to witnesses.

DIVERT WHO? I'M NOT SURE WHAT YOU MEAN.

WELL, BASICALLY I JUST...

HEY! WHAT'S THAT OVER THERE!?

WHAT?

YOINK

WHERE?

DIVERT

\di VURT\ (v.): to turn aside, to distract

To keep the child quiet during the doctor's examination, the nurse *diverted* his attention with puppets.

87

OH, WE DON'T HAVE IT! IT FELL PREY TO LARCENY CENTURIES AGO!

QUITE RIGHT. THAT WAS ABOUT THE TIME OF THE GREAT SPILLAGE!

YES, ONE OF THE SAGES OF THAT AGE SPILLED AN ENTIRE CUP OF COFFEE ON THE SACROSANCT TOME. IT WAS NEARLY ILLEGIBLE AFTER THAT, LET ME TELL YOU.

THAT WOULDN'T HAVE BEEN THE SAME TOME THAT PROMULGATED THE LEGEND OF THE TRIALS, WOULD IT...?

LARCENY

\LAR suh nee\ (n.): theft of property

The crime of stealing a wallet can be categorized as petty *larceny.*

SACROSANCT

\SAK roh sangkt\ (adj.): sacred

The president regarded his early morning exercise regimen as *sacrosanct* and refused to let anything interrupt it.

ILLEGIBLE

\ih LEJ ih bul\ (adj.): unreadable, undecipherable

Robert's handwriting was completely *illegible*, so his teachers jokingly suggested he become a doctor.

PROMULGATE

\PROM ul gayt\ (v.): to make known publicly

The publicist *promulgated* the news of the celebrity's splendid wedding to the press.

89

UNYIELDING

\un YEEL ding\ (adj.): firm, resolute

Despite her son's desperate pleas, Mrs. Young was *unyielding*: under no circumstances could he stay out after midnight.

NEGLIGIBLE

\NEG lih ju bul\ (adj.): insignificant; not worth considering

It's obvious from our *negligible* dropout rate that our students love our program.

DESOLATE

\DES uh lit\ (adj.): deserted, lifeless, barren

The *desolate* landscape in the desert left the group hungry for the plush greenery of their hometown.

GROVE

\GROHV\ (n.): a group of trees

Mark sat in the apple *grove*, surrounded by tall trees, and mulled over the week's events.

SOLITARY

\SOL ih ter ee\ (adj.): alone, unaccompanied; remote, secluded

I love going up to the mountains in the autumn to live in my *solitary* cabin in the woods.

ADVERSITY

\add VER suh tee\ (n.): a state of hardship; misfortune

The normally suspicious students gave their principal great respect, since she had risen to success despite considerable *adversity*.

WELL, TIME TO MOVE OUT. HMM, FEELS LIKE I'M FORGETTING SOMETHING...

OH, THAT'S RIGHT! I'M SUPPOSED TO BE TAKING A GIRL AROUND WITH ME, AREN'T I?

OH, MR. VAN. I'LL BE RIGHT WITH YOU... I JUST NEED... A LITTLE CATNAP... ZZZZZZ!

CATNAP

\KAT nap\ (n.): a short, light sleep

Since she had twenty minutes before her next appointment, Cheryl decided to take a *catnap* in her office.

PASSIVE

\PASS iv\ (adj.): submissive, inactive

Sheila's parents were worried that their daughter would not succeed because she was too *passive* and kept waiting for things to happen instead looking for opportunities herself.

PLAUDITS

\PLAH dits\ (n.): enthusiastic praise

After the play, Shelley walked off the stage to the *plaudits* of her classmates.

USURP

\yoo SURP\ (v.): to take over without right

The minister *usurped* the crown from the current king and had him imprisoned.

OBNOXIOUS

\ob NOK shiss\ (adj.): objectionable, offensive

Randy's *obnoxious* comments offended everyone at the party

REMOTE

\re MOHT\
(adj.): distant,
isolated

The island was
so *remote* that
Chan's cell
phone wouldn't
operate.

MEDDLER

\MED ler\
(n.): a person
interfering in
others' affairs

Mickey is a real
meddler, always
sticking his nose
where it doesn't
belong.

OOH, MAYBE AFTER STOPPING FOR BRUNCH FIRST.

SO YOU'RE ALL BY YOURSELF IN THIS REMOTE SPOT, THEN? I TAKE IT YOU'VE SENT OUT THE BIG FELLOW TO DEVOUR OUR PURSUERS?

INDEED I HAVE. HE'LL MAKE SHORT WORK OF THAT MEDDLER VON HUNTER, AND I SHALL BE ABLE TO RESTORE MY REIGN UNOPPOSED!

YOU CERTAINLY MAY...

WELL, UNLESS SOMEONE ELSE WERE TO FORCE YOU TO RELINQUISH THE EBON EYE BEFORE YOU'VE HAD A CHANCE TO USE IT.

HMM? HOW DO YOU MEAN?

RESTORE

\reh STOR\ (v.): reestablish, revive

In an attempt to *restore* the city to
its former glory, the mayor began
a campaign to clean up the streets
and attract more upscale citizens.

RELINQUISH

\re LIN kwish\ (v.): to renounce or
surrender something

The toddler was forced to
relinquish the toy when the girl
who owned it asked for it back.

TALISMAN

\TAL iss man\ (n.): a magic object that offers supernatural protection

The shop was selling *talismans* that were rumored to protect the owner from car accidents.

PROSPECT

\PROSS pekt\ (n.): possibility, chance, likelihood

The *prospect* of joining the NBA was so enticing to Stephen that he practiced for ten hours every day.

DUPLICITY

\doo PLISS ih tee\ (n.): deception, dishonesty, double-dealing

Diplomatic relations between the two superpowers were outwardly friendly, yet characterized by *duplicity*.

GRACIOUS

\GRAY shus\
(adj.): kind,
compassionate,
warm-hearted

Ms. Kirchick
proved to be a
gracious host,
welcoming her
guests warmly and
offering them tea
and cookies.

NOD

NOD

OH, WOW. I'VE... NEVER ACTUALLY HAD A FRIEND BEFORE.

WE CAN BE THE *BESTEST* FRIENDS EVER. I PROMISE, I'LL SHARE ALL MY *DARKEST* SECRETS WITH YOU!

REALLY? (SNIFF SNIFF) THAT'S SO GRACIOUS. NO ONE HAS EVER BEEN SO NICE TO ME BEFORE!

THICKET

\THIK et\ (n.):
an area filled with
dense bushes

Larry tried
catching his
neighbor's kitten
that got loose,
but it ran into the
thicket in back of
the house.

OKAY, SO INSTEAD OF SITTING AROUND THE VILLAGE AND BEING BORED, I'M HIDING IN A <u>THICKET</u> AND BEING BORED. BOREDOM SEEMS TO BE <u>INEVITABLE</u>.

INEVITABLE

\in EV ih tu bul\ (adj.): certain,
unavoidable

With an active effort to cut costs
and raise productivity, bankruptcy
is far from *inevitable*.

CHAPTER 666

(UH, YEAH...IT'S REALLY JUST CHAPTER 6.)

BARRICADE

\BAR ih kayd\ (n.): an obstacle, a barrier

During the French Revolution, students set up *barricades* in Paris to keep the army from moving through the streets.

THANKS!

FWAP

MUNCH MUNCH MUNCH MUNCH MUNCH

ANYWAY... WHAT WAS MY POINT?

OH YEAH, HE'D HAVE TO EAT THAT THOUSAND-YEAR-OLD SANDWICH INFESTED WITH *VIRULENT* *PARASITES* BEFORE HE COULD GET THE EVIL THINGAMABOB!!

THOUSAND-YEAR-OLD... SANDWICH?

YEAH.

VIRULENT

\VIR yu lint\ (adj.): extremely infectious; irritating, harsh or hateful

Alarmed at the *virulent* hate mail she was receiving, the movie star decided to hire a bodyguard.

PARASITE

\PAR uh siyt\ (n.): a person or animal that lives at another's expense

The veterinarian checked Rover, the family dog, for all manner of common infections and *parasites*.

WILY

\WHY lee\ (adj.): clever, deceptive

Yet again, the *wily* coyote managed to elude the ranchers who wanted to capture it.

RASCAL

\RAS kul\ (n.): playful, mischievous person; a scoundrel

"You little *rascals*! I'll get you for this!" shouted Mr. Wilson as Dennis and Joey ran from his broken window.

TURPITUDE

\TUR pi tood\
(n.): inherent
vileness, foulness,
depravity

The utter
turpitude of his
offenses ensured
an immediate
dismissal.

CONTEMPTUOUS

\kon TEMP shoo us\
(adj.): scornful,
disdainful

Roger shot Mary a
contemptuous look
after she insulted him
repeatedly without
cause.

...AND THEN HE TELLS ME, "YOU DON'T HAVE THE MORAL *TURPITUDE* TO BE A VAMPIRE!"

MY DAD WAS ALWAYS SO *CONTEMPTUOUS* OF ME. I TRY TO BE EVIL, I REALLY DO!

BUT NOTHING WAS *EVER* EVIL ENOUGH FOR HIM!

THIS IS WONDERFUL, IT'S SO *THERAPEUTIC* TO SHARE THESE THINGS... *SNIFF SNIFF*

NO MORE! THAT'S IT!

I THOUGHT WE WERE TALKING ABOUT BEING THE KIND OF FRIENDS WHO ENJOY THEIR *CAMARADERIE* WHILE DRINKING BEER AND TALKING ABOUT THE LADIES.

THERAPEUTIC

\ther uh PYOO tik\ (adj.): healing,
medicinal; beneficial

Trent found the hot springs to be very
therapeutic for his aches and pains, so
he bathed in them often.

CAMARADERIE

\kahm RAH da ree\ (n.):
companionship, trust; sociability
amongst friends

The photo, taken of the whole group as
they sat in a circle joking comfortably,
clearly shows their *camaraderie*.

MELODRAMA

\MEL oh drah ma\ (n.): drama
characterized by exaggerated emotions
and interpersonal conflicts

"My life is a *melodrama*!" moaned Nat
after arguing with his parents and his
best friend in the same day.

CONVERGENCE

\kun VER jinss\ (n.): the state of separate elements joining or coming together

No one in the quiet neighborhood could have predicted the mass *convergence* of artists, writers, and musicians, and the birth of a miniature renaissance.

TIMELESS

\TIYM les\ (adj.): eternal, ageless

Although some riches go out of style, the world's love for diamonds seems to be timeless.

SYNERGY

\SIN er jee\ (n.): cooperative interaction producing greater results

Improved *synergy* among the team members helped to produce a better product than the same team had developed a year earlier.

RADIANT

\RAY dee unt\ (adj.): glowing; beaming

Christopher looked back and smiled at his *radiant* bride as she walked down the aisle.

106

VENGEANCE

\VEN jinss\ (n.): retribution

While their actions against the homeowner were wrong, his act of *vengeance* was uncalled for and overdone.

AFFECTATION

\ah feck TAY shun\ (n.):
pretension, performance; false
display

In this day and age, wearing a
high lace collar and a feathered
hat to work is a rather bizarre
affectation.

BRANDISH

\BRAN dish\ (v.): to wave
menacingly

Wyatt Earp's reputation had grown
so spectacularly that by the end of
his career he could make outlaws
surrender by simply *brandishing*
his weapon.

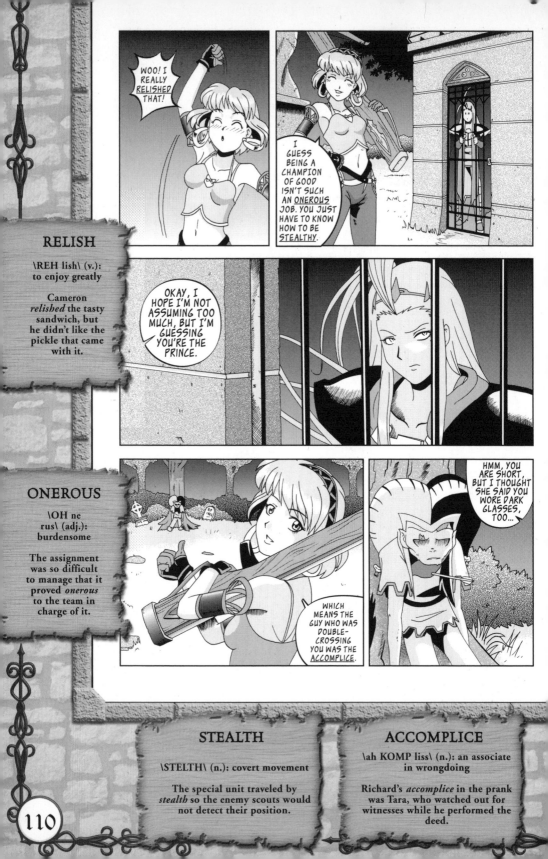

RELISH

\REH lish\ (v.):
to enjoy greatly

Cameron *relished* the tasty sandwich, but he didn't like the pickle that came with it.

ONEROUS

\OH ne rus\ (adj.): burdensome

The assignment was so difficult to manage that it proved *onerous* to the team in charge of it.

WOO! I REALLY RELISHED THAT!

I GUESS BEING A CHAMPION OF GOOD ISN'T SUCH AN ONEROUS JOB. YOU JUST HAVE TO KNOW HOW TO BE STEALTHY.

OKAY, I HOPE I'M NOT ASSUMING TOO MUCH, BUT I'M GUESSING YOU'RE THE PRINCE.

WHICH MEANS THE GUY WHO WAS DOUBLE-CROSSING YOU WAS THE ACCOMPLICE.

HMM, YOU ARE SHORT, BUT I THOUGHT SHE SAID YOU WORE DARK GLASSES, TOO...

STEALTH

\STELTH\ (n.): covert movement

The special unit traveled by *stealth* so the enemy scouts would not detect their position.

ACCOMPLICE

\ah KOMP liss\ (n.): an associate in wrongdoing

Richard's *accomplice* in the prank was Tara, who watched out for witnesses while he performed the deed.

ANTICIPATE

\an TISS uh payt\ (v.): to expect; to look forward to; to realize in advance

Although the CD was greatly *anticipated* because of the tremendous success of the artist's debut, it proved to be sadly disappointing.

EXPEDITE

\EK spe diyt\ (v.): to speed up the progress of

The lawyers worked judiciously to *expedite* the release of their client from prison.

MOROSE

\mor ROHSS\
(adj.): gloomy,
sullen, or surly

After hearing that
the university
had rejected him,
Lenny was *morose*
for weeks.

ASSURANCE

\uh SHOOR ans\ (n.): guarantee,
pledge

Roger and Joelle gave their *assurance*
to their parents that they would
clean the house before they went to
sleep.

BELLIGERENT

\be LIJ er ent\ (adj.): hostile,
inclined to fight

Although he had a reputation for
being peaceable, Gerald could
actually become quite *belligerent*
when he felt he was being mocked.

QUERULOUS

\KWER uh lus\ (adj.): irritable, complaining, grumbling

His parents were tired of his *querulous* attitude and threatened to ground him if he complained anymore that night.

PROXIMITY

\prok SIM ih tee\ (n.): nearness

Tim was careful to put the glass out of reach, since the toddler loved to yank down objects in her *proximity*.

AND AS FOR YOU!

OW! THAT BLACK-JACK THINGIE REALLY HURT!

I'M SORRY. WOULD YOU BE LESS QUERULOUS IF I HAD USED THE SPIKED MACE INSTEAD?

ER...

YOU SEEM FAMILIAR TO ME FOR SOME REASON. WHERE DO I KNOW YOU FROM?

OH, DON'T ASK ME. I HAVE AMNESIA.

THAT'S NOT REALLY A SURPRISE.

VIRTUALLY EVERYONE IN PROXIMITY TO DIKAY IS SUFFERING FROM SOME DEGREE OF MAGICALLY INDUCED AMNESIA. QUITE VEXING, REALLY.

INDUCE

\in DOOS\ (v.): to bring about; to persuade

Tom attempted to *induce* his girlfriend to go skydiving with him, but she refused.

VEX

\VEKS\ (v.): to irritate, annoy; to confuse, puzzle

The data began to *vex* the scientist; despite her many years of experience, she could not draw a single conclusion from the findings before her.

OUR LORDSHIP'S AUTHORITARIAN REIGN OF EVIL, THE EXPLOITS OF HIS LEGIONS OF TERROR, AND EVEN HIS VERY REPUTATION HAVE BEEN FORGOTTEN BY NEARLY EVERYONE. IT'S TERRIBLE!

HOLD UP FOR A SECOND. EXPLAIN TO ME HOW THAT'S TERRIBLE.

MY REIGN OF EVIL WAS ALL TOO EPHEMERAL. MY LEGIONS OF TERROR WERE DEFEATED. IF ALL MEMORY OF THAT EVAPORATES, SO MUCH THE BETTER.

ACTUALLY, I'M PRETTY SURE THOSE ARE BOTH COMMON KNOWLEDGE.

...WHERE I WILL BE KNOWN SOLELY FOR MY DESPOTISM, AND NOT FOR SOME HORRIBLE NICKNAME I HAVE BEEN SADDLED WITH FOR FAR TOO LONG.

YES... WELL... EVEN SO, I AM STARTING WITH A MOSTLY CLEAN SLATE. IT IS THE ONSET OF A NEW REIGN OF TERROR...

AUTHORITARIAN

\aw THAR ih TAYR ee on\ (adj.): demanding absolute obedience to authority

The *authoritarian* ruler forbade newspapers from criticizing his policies.

EPHEMERAL

\i FEM er il\ (adj.): momentary, transient, fleeting

The lives of mayflies seem *ephemeral* to us, since their average life span is a matter of hours.

EVAPORATE

\ee VAP uh rayt\ (v.): to vanish quickly

You need to watch the pot carefully, since the sauce will begin to burn once the water *evaporates.*

ONSET

\ON set\ (n.): the start

At the *onset* of the boxing match, the referee told the fighters that he wouldn't tolerate any foul play.

DESPOTISM

\DES puh tizm\ (n.): dominance through threat of violence

Unwilling to resort to the *despotism* of past rulers, the king granted unprecedented freedom to his people as they threatened to revolt.

115

WAVER

\WAY ver\ (v.): to move unsteadily back and forth; to hesitate, falter

After her husband *wavered* for several minutes, Mildred grew exasperated and decided to order dinner for him.

RECALL

\re KAWL\ (v.): to remember; to cancel, revoke, take back

When the car company realized that its latest model was unsafe, it was forced to *recall* fifty thousand automobiles.

HARANGUE

\hu RANG\ (n.): a pompous speech, a tirade

Although Richard's criticism of the company threatened to derail the board meeting, the chairman let him finish his *harangue* before adjourning.

SUPPLANT

\su PLANT\ (v.): to replace, substitute

After his miserable performance, the young CEO was *supplanted* by a more experienced candidate.

THE SEVENTH CHAPTER

(HEY, THAT TITLE IS SO CATCHY, WE DON'T EVEN NEED A SUBTITLE. SWEET!)

INAUSPICIOUS

\in aw SPISH is\ (adj.):
unfavorable

Telemarketers always call at the
most *inauspicious* times, like when
we sit down for dinner or when our
favorite television shows are on.

FUTILE

\FYOO tiyl\ (adj.): useless;
hopeless

"It is *futile* to resist," claimed
the invading general, "our armies
outnumber yours five to one."

INCUMBENT

\in KUM bent\ (adj.): currently holding a specified office, often political

The inexperienced candidate will need to campaign vigorously if he expects to defeat the *incumbent* senator.

EXTREME

\ek STREEM\ (adj.): very intense,
of the greatest severity

When the army officer discovered
that his unit was getting lazy,
he took *extreme* measures to get
them back into shape, instituting
mandatory weight training and
early morning runs.

DEMEANOR

\de MEE ner\ (n.): the way a
person behaves

Many psychologists believe that
a person's *demeanor* during an
interview—how they sit, where
they hold their arms, etc.—can
provide a deep insight into their
character.

CONCEITED

\kon SEET id\
(adj.): holding
an unduly high
opinion of oneself,
vain

The author was
too *conceited*
to acknowledge
that any revision
to the novel was
necessary.

WAIT! YOU'RE TAKING CREDIT? I WAS THE ONE WHO SCARED THEM OFF, YOU <u>CONCEITED EGOTIST</u>!

HMM?

OH, THAT'S RIGHT, THE BLONDE! I *KNEW* I FORGOT SOMETHING!

AH, IF IT ISN'T MY AGE-OLD <u>ADVERSARY</u>, VAN VON HUNTER.

YOU *KNOW* WHAT I'VE COME FOR.

NOW GIVE ME THE *EVIL EYE*!

EGOTIST

\EE go tist\ (n.): self-centered
person

Harvey, a known *egotist*, did not
surprise anyone when he spent
the entire evening talking about
himself.

ADVERSARY

\ADD ver SEH ree\ (n.):
opponent, enemy

Joan and her *adversary* each won
two fencing matches.

COMPLIANT

\kom PLY int\ (adj.): submissive
and yielding

Lowell always fights with his
stubborn siblings, but his friends
have more *compliant* personalities.

BENEFICIAL
\ben uh FISH ul\ (adj.):
advantageous, helpful

Mayor Bolder decided not to
increase taxes because he decided
that having more money in the
marketplace would prove to be
more *beneficial* in the long run.

CONTAMINATE
\kon TAM uh nayt\ (v.): to make
impure by contact

The scientists had to wear special
rubber suits when working in the
lab so they wouldn't *contaminate*
the delicate solution.

DETERMINE

\di TUR min\ (v.): to decide, establish

The scientists were unable to *determine* the cause of the strange ailment.

CONTRACT

\kon TRAKT\ (v.): to acquire, incur

Libby was hesitant to visit her uncle in the hospital out of a fear that she would *contract* a serious illness.

HEINOUS

\HAY nes\ (adj.): shocking,
wicked, terrible

The *heinous* crime shocked even
the most seasoned officers on the
force.

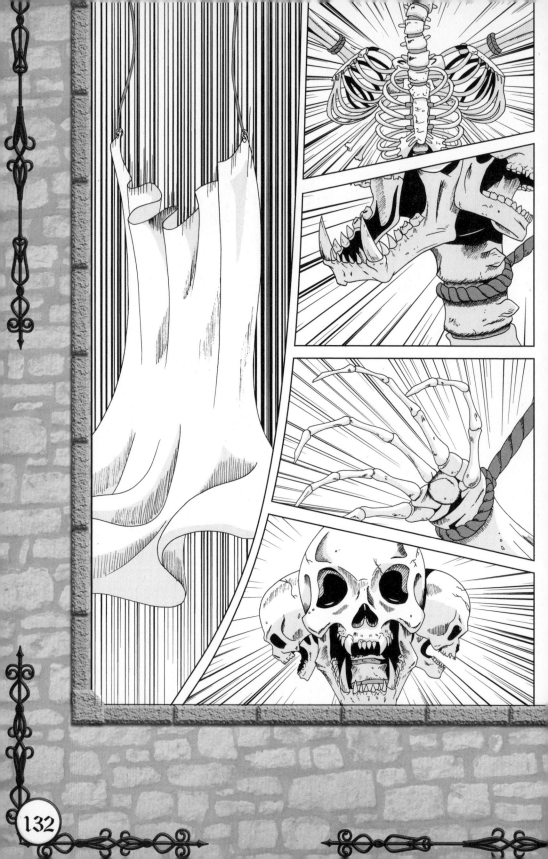

SUSPEND

\su SPEND\ (v.): to dangle, to hang; to defer, to interrupt

Construction of the building was *suspended* when the contractor ran out of bricks.

PERSPICACIOUS

\pur spi KAY shuss\ (adj.): shrewd, astute, keen-witted

Sherlock Holmes uses his *perspicacious* mind to solve mysteries.

ROUSE

\ROWZ\ (v.): provoke, excite, stir

After noticing their listless play in the previous game, the cheerleaders were determined to *rouse* the basketball team to play harder in tonight's game.

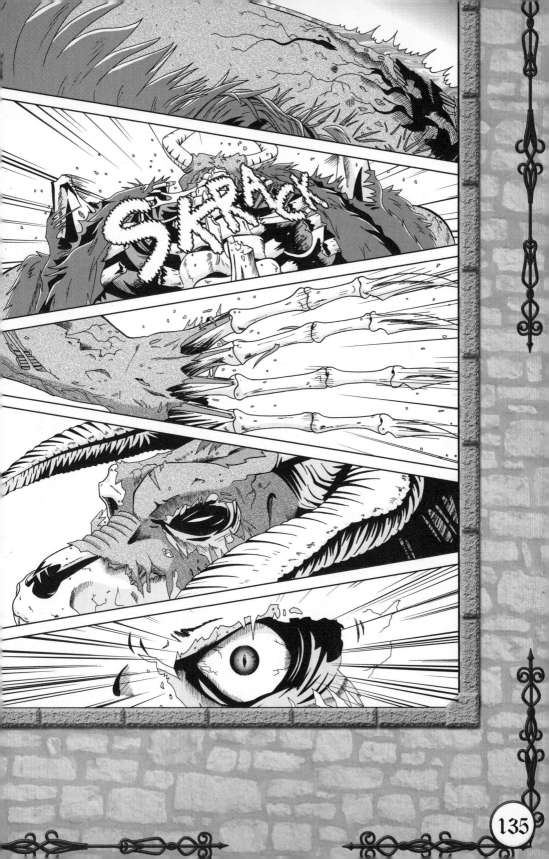

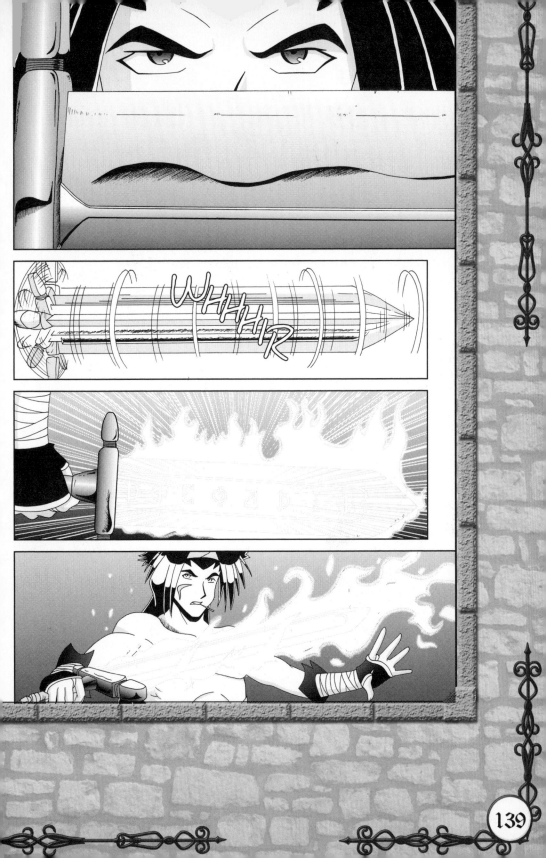

DEFT

\DEFT\ (adj.): skillful, dexterous

Mario Lemieux *deftly* skated around his opponents to score the winning goal of the game.

COMPREHENSIBLE

\kom pree HEN sih bul\ (adj.): readily understood

The publisher had to reject the author's latest novel because it was too complicated to be *comprehensible*.

HA! BOTH OF YOUR MONSTERS WERE EASILY DISPOSED OF!

THE BLACK KNICKKNACK MAY COMMAND DARK POWERS WHICH ARE NOT COMPREHENSIBLE TO MERE HUMANS, BUT IT CERTAINLY DOESN'T HAVE ENOUGH POWER TO ALLOW A WUSSY GUY LIKE YOU TO DEFEAT THE FORMIDABLE...

...VAN VON HUNTER!

FORMIDABLE

\FOR mid uh bul\ (adj.): arousing fear or dread; inspiring awe or wonder; difficult to undertake

Realizing that she faced a *formidable* task, Barbara took a deep breath and began to clean her room.

FEH! YOU HAVE NO IDEA WHAT YOU'RE TALKING ABOUT!

WITH THE BLACK MAGIC OF THE BLARBLE, I WILL BE COMPLETELY INDOMITABLE, AND MY KINGDOM SHALL ENCOMPASS THE ENTIRE WORLD!

UM, AS SOON AS I FIGURE OUT HOW TO USE IT...

INDOMITABLE

\in DOM ih tu bul\ (adj.): fearless, unconquerable

Samson was *indomitable* in battle until the treacherous Delilah cut off his hair, taking away his strength.

ENCOMPASS

\en COM pass\ (v.): to constitute, include, encircle

The syllabus for Professor Grumman's upcoming course will *encompass* all American political history, from Teddy Roosevelt to FDR.

148

FRAGILE

\FRAJ il\ (adj.): delicate, frail

Mr. Thompson didn't trust his servants with the *fragile* vase and insisted on cleaning it himself.

EXACERBATE

\ig ZAS ur bayt\ (v.): to aggravate, intensify the bad qualities of

It is unwise to take aspirin to relieve heartburn; instead of providing relief, the drug will only *exacerbate* the problem.

INDEBTED

\in DET id\ (adj.): obligated to someone else, beholden

Tommy was forever *indebted* to his neighbor for introducing him to his future wife.

ELUSIVE

\ee LOO siv\ (adj.): hard to find

Despite significant advances in theoretical physics, scientists are finding a common unifying theory for the universe to be more *elusive* than ever.

SALVAGE

\SAL vij\ (v.): to recover, save from loss

Historians have been attempting to *salvage* the remains of the Titanic for years, but attempts to raise the ship to the surface have failed.

LIBERATE

\LIB uh rayt\ (v.)—to emancipate, to set free

The politician promised to *liberate* individuals unjustly imprisoned during the current administration's tenure.

PURSUIT

\pur SOOT\ (n.): the act of chasing or striving

While the *pursuit* of happiness is a basic right afforded to citizens in this country, the law limits it when one person's rights interfere with the well-being of others.

CONTENT

\kon TENT\ (adj.): happy,
satisfied

Regine was *content* to let Amanda
handle the presentation, as long as
it was clear that both of them had
done the research.

PRUDENT

\PROOD int\ (adj.): wise,
sensible, cautious

Considering the small size of our
army, it would not be *prudent* for
us to attack right now.

VAN VON HUNTER

THIS IS VAN VON HUNTER IN HIS SUPER-
SPECIAL EVERYDAY WEAR. IT'S SUPER-
SPECIAL BECAUSE HE DOESN'T WEAR IT
EVERYDAY. IN FACT, HE ONLY DONS THIS
GARB WHEN BACK AT HIS ANCESTRAL
VAUGHN ESTATE...I MEAN, VON HUNTER
ESTATE.

THIS IS ONE OF VON HUNTER'S MANY DIFFERENT EVIL-
FIGHTING OUTFITS. NOTICE THE CAPE. IT WAS ACTUALLY
THE CLOAK OF A SHORT AND REALLY EVIL VAMPIRE THAT
HE STAKED A WHILE BACK.

UH...VAN VON HUNTER'S SIDEKICK

HERE'S, UH...VON HUNTER'S SIDEKICK
IN HER BAR WENCH OUTFIT. SHE'S BEEN
GOING TO THE SAME JOB IN THE CAVERN
TAVERN FOR THE PAST THREE YEARS. SO
AS YOU MIGHT SUSPECT, SHE HAS LOTS
OF DUPLICATES OF THIS OUTFIT IN HER
WARDROBE.

AND HERE'S...VON HUNTER'S SIDEKICK IN HER NEW
BATTLE OUTFIT. IN ACTUALITY, MANY OF THESE EVIL-
FIGHTING CLOTHES WERE PULLED OUT OF STORAGE FROM
THE LAST TIME SHE WAS AT THE VAUG, ER...VON HUNTER
ESTATE.

AMANDA BEAUMONT

HERE WE HAVE AMANDA IN HER OFFICIAL "CHAMPION OF THE VILLAGE OF KIZIK" OUTFIT. THERE NEVER WAS SUCH AN OUTFIT BEFORE AMANDA TOOK IT UPON HERSELF TO BECOME THE "CHAMPION OF THE VILLAGE OF KIZIK," I SHOULD NOTE.

AND WE CAN'T FORGET TO MENTION AMANDA'S OMINOUS CLOAK. IT INCREASES HER INTIMIDATION RATING BY +5 POINTS.

THE BEAST AND LASPO

OH, AND HERE WE HAVE THE BEAST SPORTING HIS, UH...LOIN CLOTH. BUT, IT IS A SCOTTISH LOINCLOTH. SEE, IT'S PLAID. IT'S GOT TO BE SCOTTISH...IF THERE IS SUCH A THING IN THE VON HUNTER UNIVERSE...

AND WE CAN'T FORGET POOR LASPO. I MEAN, AFTER ALL, HE'S THE MAIN VILLAIN IN THIS STORY! ER, WELL, HIM OR THAT PESKY FLAMING PRINCE...

MIRIAM PEABODY AND WALTER GOODRIGHT

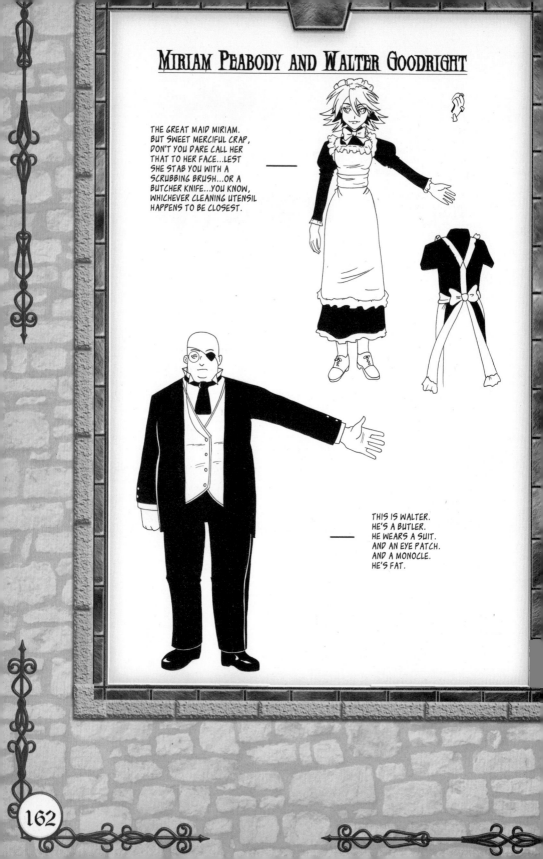

THE GREAT MAID MIRIAM.
BUT SWEET MERCIFUL CRAP,
DON'T YOU DARE CALL HER
THAT TO HER FACE...LEST
SHE STAB YOU WITH A
SCRUBBING BRUSH...OR A
BUTCHER KNIFE...YOU KNOW,
WHICHEVER CLEANING UTENSIL
HAPPENS TO BE CLOSEST.

THIS IS WALTER.
HE'S A BUTLER.
HE WEARS A SUIT.
AND AN EYE PATCH.
AND A MONOCLE.
HE'S FAT.

THE FLAMING PRINCE

HERE'S THE FLAMING PRINCE
IN HIS "I'VE BEEN DEPOSED
AND SENT INTO EXILE, BUT I
STILL WANT TO LOOK COOL
AND OMINOUS AND NOT
REMIND PEOPLE OF MY POORLY
CHOSEN MONIKER" OUTFIT.
I THINK IT ACCOMPLISHES
THAT GOAL RATHER WELL,
WOULDN'T YOU SAY?

FANART

WELCOME TO THE FANART SECTION OF THE SHOW! THE LOYAL READERSHIP AT VANVONHUNTER.COM HAS CONTRIBUTED SOME FANTASTIC STUFF THIS TIME AROUND, WHICH WE PROUDLY DISPLAY HEREIN.

BETTINA KURKOSKI

PLYMOUTH, MA

(RUNNER-UP IN *RISING STARS OF MANGA* VOL. 2 & CREATOR OF *MY CAT LOKI*)

A COMMENTARY ON THE COMPLEXITY OF
MALE/FEMALE RELATIONS, OR MUCH MORE?

BRIDGET E. WILDE
TUCSON, AZ

FLAMING PRINCE IN A RARE, INTROSPECTIVE MOMENT:
"WOW, I REALLY AM AWFULLY PRETTY."

DYNA DELESANDRI
DENTON, TX

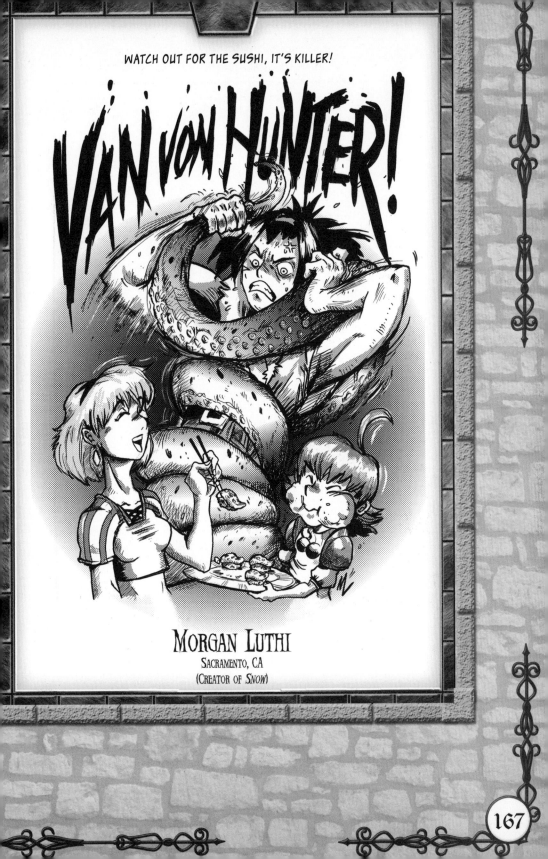

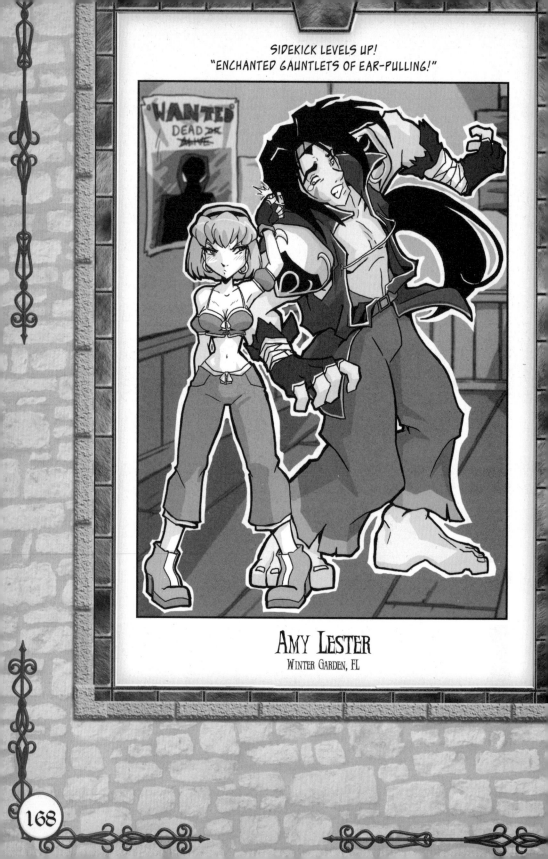

AMY LESTER

WINTER GARDEN, FL

INDEX

Boosting SAT*/ACT+ vocabulary skills has never been so much **fun!**

Millions of readers have gotten caught up in the exciting world of manga. Kaplan's *SAT/ACT Vocabulary-Building Manga* series lets you enjoy the intense excitement and fast-paced action of these edge-of-your seat graphic novels while boosting your vocabulary and preparing you to conquer the SAT and ACT exams!

Visit kaplanpublishing.com for more information on this and other great books.

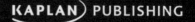

KAPLAN) PUBLISHING

www.TOKYOPOP.com

KAPLAN